I feel angry

WAYLAND

Your Emotions

I feel angry
I feel frightened
I feel jealous
I feel sad

First published in Great Britain in 1993
by Wayland (Publishers) Ltd

Wayland is a division of Hachette Children's Books,
an Hachette UK Company,
www.hachette.co.uk

Wayland
338 Euston Road, London NW1 3BH

Series edition: Mandy Suhr

British Library Cataloguing in Publication Data
Moses, Brian, 1950-
I feel angry. - (Your Emotions Series)
I. Title II. Gordon, Mike III
152.4

ISBN 978-0-7502-1403-2

27 26 25 24 23 22 21 20 19 18

Typeset by Wayland (Publishers) Ltd
Printed in China

I feel angry

Written by Brian Moses

Illustrated by Mike Gordon

WAYLAND

When I'm angry I feel like...

a volcano about
to erupt,

a saucepan about
to boil over,

a bull let loose in a china shop.

When I'm angry I feel like...
a charging rhinoceros,

a balloon about
to burst,

an exploding
firework!

7

I stamp my feet when
I'm angry ...

but it doesn't
help me very
much.

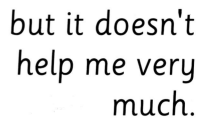

8

When I'm angry with my brother I say I won't speak to him EVER again...

but I always forgive him in the end.

When I'm angry with my friend I call her names and say I won't play with her...

but I always feel sorry later on.

All sorts of things can make people angry. When mum is tired after a hard day at work and we're making lots of noise...

then she feels
really angry!

When my sister is trying to build
a model and she just can't get
it right...

When my friend Johnny gets told off for something he hasn't done...

he feels angry.

But sometimes things that I do can make other people angry.

If I forget my manners, or I don't behave.

If I'm selfish and I won't share my toys.

If I get annoyed when
I lose at games,

or if I make fun of
someone when they
can't do something.

21

I make my teacher angry if I behave badly at school...

and cheat when I don't know
the answers to
something.

Everyone gets angry sometimes. But when I feel myself getting angry...

it helps if I count to ten before I speak.

It helps if I run until I'm puffed out, or kick a ball really hard.

It helps if I try to calm myself down.
Sometimes I tell my problems
to the dog, he seems
to understand.

And if I try to think of something nice then I often forget what I was angry about.

Our new baby can't tell anyone why he's angry but we can talk about our feelings. Saying sorry is a good place to start.

Notes for parents and teachers

Read the book with children either individually or in groups. Question them about how they feel when they get angry. Which of the ideas on pages 4-7 is the closest to how they feel, or do they picture their anger in different ways. Ask children to illustrate how they feel.

How do children behave when they are angry? Help them to compose short poems where each line begins, 'When I'm angry...'
'When I'm angry I kick my ball against the wall...'
'When I'm angry I feel my blood boil...'
'When I'm angry...etc'
This can lead into a discussion of the negative effects of some kinds of behaviour, and appropriate and inappropriate ways of behaving.

Much of the book deals with ways in which children cope with anger. Talk about how we can overcome our angry feelings, have children any personal strategies that they find useful for dealing with anger? What positive measures might be taken to remove the source of anger?

Compile a list of angry words - cross, furious, snarl, snap, fume, rage, etc. Talk about well used phrases such as, 'losing your temper', 'get in a paddy', 'throw a tantrum', 'hopping mad', etc. Children may enjoy illustrating such phrases in an amusing way.

Discuss how our own behaviour affects others. Ask children to talk or write about the things that they do that make other people angry. Are there ways that their own behaviour might change to avoid this effect on others?

Discuss how the actions of thoughtless people can rebound on others - a dog cutting it's paw on broken glass, a beauty spot ruined by litter, etc. Would these kinds of things make you angry?

Explore the notion of anger further through the sharing of picture books and poems mentioned in the book list on page 32.

These ideas will satisfy a number of Attainment Targets in the National Curriculum Guidelines for English at Key Stage 1.

Books to read

The Bad Tempered Ladybird by Eric Carle, (Picture Puffin, 1982). The Bad Tempered Ladybird thinks that it is bigger and better than anyone.

Angry Arthur by Hiawyn Oram, (Red Fox, 1993). Arthur isn't allowed to watch his favourite television programme and some surprising things happen when he gets really angry.

Little Monster by Barry Wade, (Mammoth,1991). Mandy is normally well behaved but she becomes very angry when her mother appears to favour her naughty little brother.

A Difficult Day by Eugeine Fernandes, (Kids Can Press, 2002). Melinda wakes up late and feels very grumpy, but a difficult day ends happily after all.

A first poetry book selected by John Foster, (OUP, 1979). Includes 'The Quarrel' by Eleanor Farjeon.